A LIFEGUIDE  BIBLE STUDY

PARABLES

The Greatest Stories Ever Told

*12 Studies
for individuals or groups*

John White

With Notes for Leaders

INTERVARSITY PRESS
DOWNERS GROVE, ILLINOIS 60515

InterVarsity Press® is the book-publishing division of InterVarsity Christian Fellowship®, a student movement active on campus at hundreds of universities, colleges and schools of nursing in the United States of America, and a member movement of the International Fellowship of Evangelical Students. For information about local and regional activities, write Public Relations Dept., InterVarsity Christian Fellowship, 6400 Schroeder Rd., P.O. Box 7895, Madison, WI 53707-7895.

LifeGuide® is a registered trademark of InterVarsity Christian Fellowship.

All Scripture quotations, unless otherwise indicated, are taken from the HOLY BIBLE, NEW INTERNATIONAL VERSION®. NIV®. Copyright ©1973, 1978, 1984 by International Bible Society. Used by permission of Zondervan Publishing House. All rights reserved.

Cover photograph: Peter French

ISBN 0-8308-1037-4

Printed in the United States of America ♾

27	26	25	24	23	22	21	20	19	18	17	16	15	14	13	12	11	10
10	09	08	07	06	05	04	03	02	01	00	99	98	97	96	95	94	

Contents

Getting the Most
from LifeGuide Bible Studies

Many of us long to fill our minds and our lives with Scripture. We desire to be transformed by its message. LifeGuide Bible Studies are designed to be an exciting and challenging way to do just that. They help us to be guided by God's Word in every area of life.

How They Work

LifeGuides have a number of distinctive features. Perhaps the most important is that they are *inductive* rather than *deductive*. In other words, they lead us to *discover* what the Bible says rather than simply *telling* us what it says.

They are also thought provoking. They help us to think about the meaning of the passage so that we can truly understand what the author is saying. The questions require more than one-word answers.

The studies are personal. Questions expose us to the promises, assurances, exhortations and challenges of God's Word. They are designed to allow the Scriptures to renew our minds so that we can be transformed by the Spirit of God. This is the ultimate goal of all Bible study.

The studies are versatile. They are designed for student, neighborhood and church groups. They are also effective for individual study.

How They're Put Together

LifeGuides also have a distinctive format. Each study need take no more than forty-five minutes in a group setting or thirty minutes in personal study—unless you choose to take more time.

The studies can be used within a quarter system in a church and fit well in a semester or trimester system on a college campus. If a guide has more than thirteen studies, it is divided into two or occasionally three parts of approximately twelve studies each.

LifeGuides use a workbook format. Space is provided for writing answers to each question. This is ideal for personal study and allows group members to prepare in advance for the discussion.

The studies also contain leader's notes. They show how to lead a group discussion, provide additional background information on certain questions, give helpful tips on group dynamics and suggest ways to deal with problems which may arise during the discussion. With such helps, someone with little or no experience can lead an effective study.

Suggestions for Individual Study

1. As you begin each study, pray that God will help you to understand and apply the passage to your life.

2. Read and reread the assigned Bible passage to familiarize yourself with what the author is saying. In the case of book studies, you may want to read through the entire book prior to the first study. This will give you a helpful overview of its contents.

3. A good modern translation of the Bible, rather than the King James Version or a paraphrase, will give you the most help. The New International Version, the New American Standard Bible and the Revised Standard Version are all recommended. However, the questions in this guide are based on the New International Version.

4. Write your answers in the space provided in the study guide. This will help you to express your understanding of the passage clearly.

5. It might be good to have a Bible dictionary handy. Use it to look up any unfamiliar words, names or places.

Suggestions for Group Study

1. Come to the study prepared. Follow the suggestions for individual study mentioned above. You will find that careful preparation will greatly enrich your time spent in group discussion.

2. Be willing to participate in the discussion. The leader of your group will not be lecturing. Instead, he or she will be encouraging the members of the group to discuss what they have learned from the passage. The leader will be asking the questions that are found in this guide. Plan to share what God has taught you in your individual study.

3. Stick to the passage being studied. Your answers should be based on the verses which are the focus of the discussion and not on outside authorities such as commentaries or speakers. This guide deliberately avoids jumping from book to book or passage to passage. Each study focuses on only one passage. Book studies are generally designed to lead you through the book in the order in which it was written. This will help you follow the author's argument.

4. Be sensitive to the other members of the group. Listen attentively when they share what they have learned. You may be surprised by their insights! Link what you say to the comments of others so the group stays on the topic. Also, be affirming whenever you can. This will encourage some of the more hesitant members of the group to participate.

5. Be careful not to dominate the discussion. We are sometimes so eager to share what we have learned that we leave too little opportunity for others to respond. By all means participate! But allow others to also.

6. Expect God to teach you through the passage being discussed and through the other members of the group. Pray that you will have an enjoyable and profitable time together.

7. If you are the discussion leader, you will find additional suggestions and helpful ideas for each study in the leader's notes. These are found at the back of the guide.

Introducing Parables

In Texas people love to tell "Aggie jokes." (Aggies are students at Texas A & M University—an excellent institution.) A group of Aggies were at a camp one summer with students from other schools. They were the butt of so many jokes that they finally gave an ultimatum: "The next person who tells an Aggie joke gets thrown into the stream!" Everything was quiet for several days. Then one morning the camp director got up as usual to report on current news items. When he got to the local news he said: "Several Texas A & M students were seriously injured this week while drinking milk." (At this point everyone tensed with anticipation.) "It's reported that the cow fell on them!" As shouts of laughter filled the room, the Aggies shot up out of their seats. They grabbed the camp director, dragged him outside kicking and screaming, and tossed him in the icy mountain stream.

In a sense parables are like jokes. They are designed to catch people off guard and to elicit an immediate response. Parables "capture the listener and make him a participant, overturning his world view and leading him to call into question his most basic values."[1] If a parable has to be explained, it loses much of its force, just as a joke does when someone doesn't get it and needs an explanation.[2]

For this reason we are at somewhat of a disadvantage in studying the parables. Unlike the original hearers, who usually understood the context and points of reference in the parables, we often miss the point. Of course we can discover the point by understanding the cultural and literary context of the parable. But the element of surprise, the unexpected twist which catches us off guard, is gone.

Nevertheless, there is great value in studying the parables. They illustrate some of Jesus' most important teachings. And they demand crucial responses from us, just as they did from those who first heard them.

In order to gain the greatest benefit from the parables, we must understand what they are and how they function.

A parable is an extended metaphor or illustration. It is an illustration turned into a tale, a tale elaborated on the spur of the moment by a gifted teacher. And Jesus was a supremely gifted teacher. Accustomed to preaching to a crowd with a wide range of understanding and attitudes, he based each parable on the common, everyday events that made up first-century life—lost money, sheep and shepherds, cruel creditors.

Like most illustrations, parables usually have one central point. They differ from allegories, stories in which the details abound with hidden meanings. Failure to distinguish between parables and allegories, and the attempt to treat the parables of Jesus as though they were allegories, has led some Bible students far afield, pursuing mysterious meanings in meaningless details.

Both Christ's teaching and his parables focus on the issue of kingdom. Kingdom in the gospels does not have to do with territory or realm ruled over, but with the rule or authority itself—God's rule on earth in the person of Christ. Jesus demonstrated that kingdom authority over disease, demons, nature, and supremely over sin and death. And in his preaching and parables he revealed the standards and values of the kingdom. These contrast sharply with the values and standards of contemporary society.

So parables brilliantly illustrate important truths about Christ's kingdom, truths which demand a response. But the sad fact is that our rebellion and sin often close our minds and hinder our response. Thus the brilliance of the illustration may only cause some people to persist all the more deeply in error. In our first parable we will get a chance to look at this sad fact.

This guide introduces you to several of Jesus' parables and their application for today. It is my prayer that you will be captivated and challenged by the parables, that you will have "ears to hear" what the Lord is saying to you through them.

[1]D. A. Carson gives this brief summary of A. Thiselton's view of parables in *Matthew,* The Expositor's Bible Commentary, vol. 8, ed. Frank E. Gaebelien (Grand Rapids, Mich.: Zondervan, 1984), p. 302.

[2]This comparison is made by Gordon Fee and Douglas Stuart in *How to Read the Bible for All Its Worth* (Grand Rapids, Mich.: Zondervan, 1982), pp. 123-34. This book contains an excellent chapter on the parables.

1
Parable of the Sower
Matthew 13:1-23

Have you ever wondered why the same book or the same sermon will produce strikingly different results in different people? How is it, for instance, that some people seem unable to grasp the simplest and most obvious spiritual truths while others are transformed by them? Jesus' most important parable tells why.

I call it his "most important" because it provides more clues than any other parable as to the nature of parables and how they should be interpreted. The parable is followed by Christ's own interpretation and discussion of its contents. It is an excellent place to begin our study of the parables.

---

1. Why are some people more open to spiritual things than others?

Some Are searching, some have Been Brought up in A christian environment.

---

2. Read Matthew 13:1-23. How was this parable well-suited to the personal experiences of the crowds gathered around Jesus (vv. 1-9)?

most all could relate to A Farmer & understand the conditions of the environment

3. In verse 10 the disciples ask Jesus, "Why do you speak to the people in parables?" How would you summarize his answer (vv. 11-16)?

Because they didn't know about Heaven, it gave them something to relate with so they could understand.

4. How do parables help Jesus' followers understand his kingdom but hinder the understanding of those who don't follow him closely (vv. 12-17)?

5. In verses 18-23 Jesus explains the meaning of this parable to his disciples. The seed is the message of the kingdom (v. 19). Who is the farmer, and who is the soil?

6. Satanic "birds" destroyed the value of God's word for the first group of people. Why? What did these hearers lack (v. 19)?

An open heart to listen to God's gentle tugging. They were closer-minded.

7. What can we do to help people understand God's message?

Make it simple. We tend to get churchy with these people

8. Verses 20-21 describe the kind of person referred to as stony or

rocky soil. What examples have you seen of people who respond this
way? *They Are on Fire For the Lord but As
soon As trouble Arises, they usually BlAme or
question God instead of trying to understand
God's Leading*

9. How can we avoid this in our own lives and discourage it in the
lives of others? *Get into God's word, be in constant pray*
w/Him.
B. show them examples From the bible of christian

10. What kind of person does the third type of soil describe (v. 22)?
worrier or the person concerned About
Themselves. The "I" syndrome.

11. How can we avoid being choked by the weeds and thorns Jesus
mentions (v. 23)?
Give everything to God.
Get into His word - understand it:
constant commune w/ God.

12. Which of the four kinds of soil do you most identify with? Explain.
Thorns - I have A problem with worrying. I
usually give something to God, but more times than
NOT, I take it back & worry about the solution.

13. What are some practical examples of how we can become "good
soil" (v. 23)?
Confess to God & others.
Be Accountable to somebody
Be involved in church groups

2
The Lost Sheep, the Lost Coin and the Lost Son

Luke 15:1-32

"If people really knew me, they would reject me." To avoid this risk, we often wear masks we think people will like. We hide who we really are, putting ourselves under constant strain.

We often feel this same way about God. We think we are rejected and condemned rather than welcomed and loved. We do our best to please him but feel that we never measure up. In these three parables Jesus sets us straight about God's attitude toward sinners. The result is a startling picture of God.

1. In each of the following pairs of words, which one more accurately describes your image of who God is? Somber or joyous? Searching or waiting? Welcoming or judging? Explain your answers.

2. Read Luke 15:1-32. What bothered the Pharisees and teachers of the law (the Jewish religious leaders), and why (vv. 1-2)?

3. When do you find yourself bothered by other Christians in a similar way today?

4. When reading stories or parables, it helps to imagine the sights, sounds, smells and feelings. What comes to mind when you read the parables of the lost sheep and the lost coin (vv. 4-10)?

5. Who is represented by the central characters (or objects) in each of the three parables?

6. How do you account for the intense reactions of the shepherd, woman and father to their losses and to their finds?

7. Describe an incident when you lost or misplaced something valuable to you. How did you feel?

8. Let's look more closely at the third parable. How might the Pharisees and teachers of the law have felt about each of the actions of the younger son (vv. 13-16)?

9. How might they have expected the father to respond when the son returned home?

10. What do the details in verses 20-24 reveal about the feelings of our Father in heaven?

11. How can this portrait of God help us to feel fully accepted by the Father—in spite of our sin?

12. Instead of concluding the story in verse 24, Jesus goes on to describe the reaction of the older son (vv. 25-32). What additional point do you think Jesus wants to make to the Jewish leaders, and why?

13. How can this parable motivate us to seek those who are lost?

3
The Good Samaritan

Luke 10:25-37

What makes a neighbor? Geographical proximity? Community of race or religion? Sharing the same social or economic level? In this parable Jesus overturns our traditional definitions and shatters our stereotypes of what it means to be a neighbor to those around us.

1. Do you feel guilty when you see pictures of starving people on TV or in magazines? Should you? Explain.

2. Read Luke 10:25-37. Do you think the law expert's first question was sincere? Why or why not?

What about his second question? Explain.

3. In what sense did the expert in the law "correctly" answer his own question (vv. 27-28)?

---

4. Legalists are sometimes defined as people who try to scale down God's law to justify their own behavior. Do you think the expert in the law is guilty of this (v. 29)? Why or why not?

In what ways have you discovered this tendency in yourself?

---

5. The situation described in verse 30 was common on the dangerous road from Jerusalem to Jericho. In what situations today is noninvolvement seen as a wise choice?

---

6. Why do you suppose Jesus picked a Samaritan, someone from an ethnic group Jews detested, as the "hero" of the story (vv. 31-33)?

---

7. Describe the Samaritan's actions from the point of view of (a) personal inconvenience, (b) financial cost and (c) risk (vv. 34-35).

How big a factor is each of these in discouraging your own neighborly actions? Any examples?

8. Christ's question (v. 36) was not intended to prove that Samaritans could be better neighbors than Jews. What was he getting at?

9. "Go and do likewise" (v. 37). What exactly was Jesus telling the expert in the law to do?

10. In what practical ways can we "go and do likewise" today?

4
The Unforgiving Servant

Matthew 18:15, 21-35

I t seems to be true (at a psychological level anyway) that a critical, unforgiving person tends also to be a guilt-prone person. And vice versa. People who struggle with guilt feelings are usually critical of others and tend to harbor resentment.

In this parable Jesus teaches the consequences of unforgiveness with brutal clarity. Unforgiveness in someone who has never experienced God's forgiveness may be understandable. But what can we say about an unforgiving Christian?

1. Why do you think people who struggle with guilt are usually critical and resentful?

2. Read Matthew 18:15, 21-35. What is the ultimate goal we should have when we approach a brother who has sinned against us?

What difficulties would you have in obeying this command?

3. In verse 21, do you think Peter's problem is actual or merely theoretical? Explain.

4. What view of forgiveness does Peter's question reveal?

5. Jesus tells Peter to forgive his brother seventy-seven times (v. 22). What is Jesus' point?

6. Ten thousand talents (v. 24) was equal to several million dollars. The king's intended action (v. 25) represented contemporary justice. If you were the man, how would you have felt before and after the king canceled your debt (vv. 25-27)?

7. How real to you is (a) your indebtedness to God? (b) the marvel of your escape from justice? Explain.

8. A hundred denarii (v. 28) is a trivial amount compared to ten thousand talents. What lesson do you think Christ intends by the sum?

How should the comparison of the two sums affect our view of the sins of others?

9. Think of someone you have had difficulty forgiving. How would it help to compare their actions to what God has forgiven you for?

10. What can we conclude about those who profess the faith yet do not forgive?

11. What happens to our spiritual freedom and our fellowship with God when we are critical and unforgiving (vv. 34-35)?

12. Take time to thank God for his forgiveness. Ask his help in forgiving those who have hurt or mistreated you.

5
The Widow and the Judge

Luke 18:1-8

Today many people are suffering from a disease known as "lottery fever," the gambling craze sparked by million-dollar lotteries. Week by week two or three winners are interviewed on TV, keeping the fever high. Yet logically a person's chances of winning are very small, so small that you would think people would soon get discouraged. Yet millions go on playing the lotteries unsuccessfully all their lives. They never lose hope.

But Christians who pray often do. Why? What makes us give up when the answer delays? Why do many of us stop expecting anything when we pray, using "Thy will be done" as an excuse for unbelief? In this parable Jesus tells us why we should always pray and never give up.

1. Is there as much excitement and expectancy in your prayers now as there was when you first became a Christian? Why or why not?

2. Read Luke 18:1-8. In your opinion, what are the key words in verse 1? Explain your answer.

3. The characters in the parable are drawn sketchily but vividly. What images come to mind when you think about the widow? The judge?

4. Why do you think the widow is so persistent?

5. What finally motivates the judge to act (vv. 4-5)?

6. What we believe about God and how we *feel* about him when we pray may not be the same. For example, I may believe God cares for all my needs, but I may feel resentful that he hasn't helped me get a job. In what ways do your feelings and beliefs sometimes conflict when you pray?

7. Use your imagination to fill in the details about those praying to God in verses 6-8. How would you describe them and their circumstances?

8. Are your prayers as desperate as those described here? Why or why not?

9. In what ways can we expect God to do far more for those in verse 7 than the judge did for the widow?

10. Jesus told this parable to show us that we should always pray and not give up (v. 1). How would you explain the uncertainty of his final question in verse 8?

11. When are you most tempted to give up praying about someone or something?

12. How can this parable encourage you to keep on praying?

13. Think of one or two areas where you are discouraged and ready to give up praying. Ask God to help you to be persistent in prayer.

6
The Wheat
and the Weeds
Matthew 13:24-30, 36-43

W e all wish God would remove evil from the world. But put
yourself in God's place for a moment: if by a simple word of power
you could snatch evil doers away from earth, what complications might
arise from your decision? As one person has said, "If God were to
destroy all evil at midnight, who would be left at one o'clock?" In this
parable Jesus tells us why God allows good and evil to coexist in the
world.

1. Have you ever been frustrated by the fact that God has not yet
removed all evil from the world? Explain.

2. Read Matthew 13:24-30, 36-43. What crisis occurs at the beginning
of the parable (vv. 24-26)?

3. The owner's servants offer to pull up the weeds (v. 28). What alternative does the owner propose, and why (vv. 29-30)?

4. According to Jesus, what do the key elements of the parable stand for (vv. 37-39)?

5. What does the enemy's activity in this parable tell us about the devil's plan and influence in the world?

6. In what sense are non-Christians "enemy agents"?

How should this affect our attitude toward them?

7. How does Jesus interpret the weeds being pulled up and burned in the fire (vv. 40-43)?

Who is given this responsibility (vv. 41-42)?

8. Like the owner's servants, how have Christians sometimes offered to pull up the weeds prematurely?

What have been some of the consequences of this misguided concern?

9. Christians have often misinterpreted the field as the church rather than the world. How would interpreting the field as the church alter the meaning of the parable?

10. How does this parable help you understand God's patience and plan for dealing with evil?

11. What hope does the parable offer us as Christians?

7
The Parable of the Vineyard Workers
Matthew 19:16—20:16

Y ou deserve the best." "Demand your rights." "I'm worth it." People today want everything that's coming to them, and they want it *now*. Convinced of our own worth, we demand higher paying jobs, better working conditions and more fringe benefits. If these are denied, we feel we have been treated unfairly—and perhaps our feelings are justified.

But what happens when we treat God like a divine employer? In this passage Jesus challenges our human concepts of fairness and worth. He shows us that kingdom values are often the opposite of what we expect.

---

1. In your opinion, what factors should determine a person's wages or salary?

---

2. Read Matthew 19:16-30. Before answering the young man's question (v. 16), Jesus asks a question of his own (v. 17). Why?

3. Jesus replies, "If you want to enter life, obey the commandments" (v. 17). If the New Testament teaches that we cannot be saved by obeying the law, then what does Jesus mean?

4. The young man implies that he has kept all ten commandments (v. 20). How do verses 21-22 make plain that that he hasn't and expose his true spiritual condition?

What value would you see in following Jesus' model here as you present the gospel to non-Christians?

5. In biblical times people thought wealth was a reward for righteousness. How does Jesus challenge this view (vv. 23-26)?

According to this passage, what hope do people have of being saved?

6. Read 20:1-16. How does this parable arise out of the discussion over the rich young man (see especially 19:27-30 and 20:16)?

Imagine that you had "borne the burden of the work and the heat of the day" yet were paid the same as those who only worked an hour. How would you feel, and why?

7. How do the landowner's wage policies compare with contemporary management policies?

How might modern union officials react to it?

8. Although the landowner's actions *seem* unfair, he claims they are not (vv. 13-15). Why aren't they unfair?

9. The landlord clearly represents God. How do his values as seen in this parable conflict with society's values?

Why is it so hard to live by these values of God?

10. How does this passage place our service to God in proper perspective?

11. Spend time thanking God for his fairness and generosity.

8
The Wise and Foolish Virgins
Matthew 24:36—25:13

The Mexican government was aware that an earthquake could happen, but preparations were not made. The Colombian government knew a volcanic eruption was imminent, but thousands lost their lives when the eruption came.

Christ's second coming is spoken of with joy from many pulpits. But for many it will be a catastrophe of unparalleled magnitude. Why do human beings unthinkingly play Russian roulette with possible disaster? This parable helps us to understand.

---

1. Give an example of a warning you may have ignored. Did ignoring the warning get harder or easier as time went on? Explain.

---

2. Read Matthew 24:36—25:13. How will the coming of the Son of Man be similar to the days of Noah (vv. 36-41)?

3. Christ's main point is not to warn against "eating and drinking, marrying and giving in marriage" (v. 38 and also v. 49). What then is he emphasizing?

4. Jesus compares his coming to a thief breaking into a house (vv. 42-44) and a master returning home (vv. 45-51). What does each story emphasize about (a) the nature of the Lord's return and (b) our responsibility?

5. If the Lord returned today, what would he hope to find us doing (vv. 45-46)?

6. In the verses we've just looked at (vv. 36-51), would you say Christ's illustrations about his coming were joyful or fearful events? Explain.

7. In biblical times the bridegroom would come to the bride's home after dark where the bridesmaids (virgins) were also waiting, and then would take her (and them) in procession to his home for the wedding feast. What are the similarities between the wise and foolish virgins (vv. 1-5)?

8. How did the bridegroom's long delay reveal the differences between the wise and foolish virgins (vv. 6-12)?

9. According to this parable what constitutes wisdom in relation to Christ's return?

10. It has been nearly two thousand years since Jesus promised to return (note v. 5). What negative effects might this have on us?

11. What can we do to overcome these negative effects and take Christ's warnings more seriously?

9
Parable of the Talents
Matthew 25:14-30

Men are *not* born equal—or women either. We live in an imperfect world. And sometimes the inequalities can seem unfair. Our sense of injustice arises from two related sources. First, as children we may fear that our parents love our brothers and sisters more than us. Then we enter a fiercely competitive world where people admire the successful. We may feel it unfair that we have fewer gifts or opportunities than those who wind up more famous or rich than we. This parable gives us a glimpse of the issues of inequality and fairness in God's kingdom.

1. If someone loaned you a million dollars and you had to pay it back in ten years, what would you do with it?

2. Read Matthew 25:14-30. A talent was not a personal ability but a measure of money equal to thousands of dollars. How and why does the master entrust his money to these servants (vv. 14-15)?

---

3. If you had been the third servant, how would you have felt about receiving only one talent when the others had more?

4. How might our envy or resentment of other Christians inhibit our faithful execution of our responsibilities?

5. Compare the reaction of the master to the first and second servants (vv. 19-23). What matters to him, and what does *not* matter?

6. As you look at the statements of the three servants (vv. 20, 22, 24-25), what can you infer about their relationships with their master?

How might their relationships have affected their actions in verses 16-18?

7. Think of people you have done jobs for. What bearing did your relationship with them have on your attitude toward the job?

8. How is the master like God and unlike God?

9. How does our relationship with God affect our attitudes toward what we do?

10. Do you think of yourself as a five-talent person, a two-talent person or a one-talent person? Explain.

11. How can you faithfully handle the responsibilities God has given you?

10
The Pharisee and the Tax Collector

Luke 18:9-14

Prayer is a kind of litmus test of our relationship with God. Our prayers reveal who and what is most important to us. They expose our innermost feelings about ourselves and about God. In this parable we overhear the prayers of two men. If we listen closely, we can discover not only how God views their prayers but ours as well.

1. What does your mind focus on when you pray?

2. Read Luke 18:9-14. How would you describe those for whose benefit Jesus tells this story (v. 9)?

3. The Pharisee addresses God, but to what extent does God occupy his attention? Explain.

4. On what positive and negative facts about himself does the Pharisee depend (vv. 11-12)?

What does this reveal about his attitude to himself and to God?

5. How many times does the Pharisee compare himself with others (v. 11)?

What does it do to you when you compare yourself with those you look down on?

6. How does the way the tax collector views himself (v. 13) contrast with the Pharisee?

7. Notice the positions, postures and gestures of the Pharisee and the tax collector. What conclusions can we draw from these contrasts in their body language?

8. What different positions have you adopted when praying?

What differences have you noticed while praying in these positions?

9. In the first century, Pharisees were viewed with great respect, while tax collectors were despised as traitors. Why then was the tax collector justified rather than the Pharisee (v. 14)?

10. In what ways are we tempted to exalt ourselves today?

11. How can we humble ourselves in our attitudes and actions?

11
Parable of the Rich Fool
Luke 12:13-21

The last parts of us to be converted are our pockets and purses. Many of us are so secretive about our feelings on the subject of money that we have concealed them even from ourselves in our unconscious minds. Unconsciously we yearn for more material things, while consciously we think we want Christ's kingdom. This parable illustrates a tension in the heart of every Christian, a tension affecting poor and rich alike. How do we resolve the conflict between our desires for earthly and heavenly treasure, earthly and heavenly security, kingdom values and the values of the world?

1. Why do you think people place such value on money and material possessions?

2. Read Luke 12:13-21. People often asked rabbis for decisions about disputed points of law. Describe everything we know or can infer about the man who comes to Jesus (vv. 13-15).

3. What should our attitude be toward greed, and why (v. 15)?

4. How would you evaluate the *actions* of the rich man in verses 16-18?

5. How would you evaluate his *attitude* in verse 19?

6. During times of prosperity, why is it easy to feel secure and at ease?

7. How does God expose the man's false sense of security (v. 20)?

8. How does this parable illustrate that "a man's life does not consist in the abundance of his possessions"?

9. Is Jesus condemning material prosperity in this parable (v. 21)? Explain.

Do you think it is possible to be prosperous without being greedy? If so, how?

10. What does it mean to be "rich toward God" (v. 21)?

11. What could the man have done to increase his spiritual wealth?

12. What practical steps can you take to become spiritually rich?

12
The Rich Man and Lazarus
Luke 16:19-31

Have you ever been embarrassed by Karl Marx's statement that religion is the opiate of the people? True religion is not the opiate of the people, since it demands that we feed the hungry and clothe the poor. Nor does true religion teach passive suffering in the face of injustice and oppression. Yet this parable reminds us all that pain and suffering in this life *can* be replaced by bliss in the next—and this hope need never embarrass us. It also teaches that wealth and power in this life do not guarantee them in the next.

1. Have you ever been accosted by a panhandler? How did you react?

2. Read Luke 16:19-31. How does this parable reveal the rich man's lack of concern for Lazarus (vv. 19-21)?

3. How would you account for his indifference toward Lazarus?

How do some rich people explain the poverty of the poor?

---

4. How do you feel when you are low on money and when you are flush with cash?

---

5. How does the parable contrast the state of the two men before their death, at their burial and after their death?

---

6. Does this parable teach that Lazarus experienced heavenly bliss *because of* his earthly poverty? Explain.

Likewise, did the rich man experience torment simply because he had been wealthy on earth? Explain.

7. Contrast the rich man's accessibility to Lazarus in life and death (vv. 20, 23, 26).

8. What is the one thing Abraham asks the rich man to do (v. 25)?

Think of a past mistake you deeply regret. How does the memory affect you?

9. Why does God not send messengers from the dead to warn us (v. 31)?

10. Why did Jesus' resurrection fail to convince people of his day, and why does it still fail to convince people today?

11. If we choose to listen (v. 31), what are Moses, the prophets and this parable saying to us?

Leader's Notes

Leading a Bible discussion can be an enjoyable and rewarding experience. But it can also be *scary*—especially if you've never done it before. If this is your feeling, you're in good company. When God asked Moses to lead the Israelites out of Egypt, he replied, "O Lord, please send someone else to do it!" (Ex 4:13).

When Solomon became king of Israel, he felt the task was far beyond his abilities. "I am only a little child and do not know how to carry out my duties. . . . Who is able to govern this great people of yours?" (1 Kings 3:7, 9).

When God called Jeremiah to be a prophet, he replied, "Ah, Sovereign LORD, . . . I do not know how to speak; I am only a child" (Jer 1:6).

The list goes on. The apostles were "unschooled, ordinary men" (Acts 4:13). Timothy was young, frail and frightened. Paul's "thorn in the flesh" made him feel weak. But God's response to all of his servants—including you—is essentially the same: "My grace is sufficient for you" (2 Cor 12:9). Relax. God helped these people in spite of their weaknesses, and he can help you in spite of your feelings of inadequacy.

There is another reason why you should feel encouraged. Leading a Bible discussion is not difficult if you follow certain guidelines. You don't need to be an expert on the Bible or a trained teacher. The suggestions listed below should enable you to effectively and enjoyably fulfill your role as leader.

Preparing to Lead

1. Ask God to help you understand and apply the passage to your own life. Unless this happens, you will not be prepared to lead others. Pray too for the various members of the group. Ask God to give you an enjoyable and profitable time together studying his Word.

2. As you begin each study, read and reread the assigned Bible passage to familiarize yourself with what the author is saying. In the case of book studies, you may want to read through the entire book prior to the first study. This will give you a helpful overview of its contents.

3. This study guide is based on the New International Version of the Bible. It will help you and the group if you use this translation as the basis for your study and discussion. Encourage others to use the NIV also, but allow them the freedom to use whatever translation they prefer.

4. Carefully work through each question in the study. Spend time in meditation and reflection as you formulate your answers.

5. Write your answers in the space provided in the study guide. This will help you to express your understanding of the passage clearly.

6. It might help you to have a Bible dictionary handy. Use it to look up any unfamiliar words, names or places. (For additional help on how to study a passage, see chapter five of *Leading Bible Discussions,* IVP.)

7. Once you have finished your own study of the passage, familiarize yourself with the leader's notes for the study you are leading. These are designed to help you in several ways. First, they tell you the purpose the study guide author had in mind while writing the study. Take time to think through how the study questions work together to accomplish that purpose. Second, the notes provide you with additional background information or comments on some of the questions. This information can be useful if people have difficulty understanding or answering a question. Third, the leader's notes can alert you to potential problems you may encounter during the study.

8. If you wish to remind yourself of anything mentioned in the leader's notes, make a note to yourself below that question in the study.

Leading the Study

1. Begin the study on time. Unless you are leading an evangelistic Bible study, open with prayer, asking God to help you to understand and apply the passage.

2. Be sure that everyone in your group has a study guide. Encourage them to prepare beforehand for each discussion by working through the questions in the guide.

3. At the beginning of your first time together, explain that these studies are meant to be discussions not lectures. Encourage the members of the group to participate. However, do not put pressure on those who may be hesitant to speak during the first few sessions.

4. Read the introductory paragraph at the beginning of the discussion. This will orient the group to the passage being studied.

5. Read the passage aloud if you are studying one chapter or less. You may choose to do this yourself, or someone else may read if he or she has been asked to do so prior to the study. Longer passages may occasionally be read in parts at different times during the study. Some studies may cover several chapters. In such cases reading aloud would probably take too much time, so the group members should simply read the assigned passages prior to the study.

6. As you begin to ask the questions in the guide, keep several things in mind. First, the questions are designed to be used just as they are written. If you wish, you may simply read them aloud to the group. Or you may prefer to express them in your own words. However, unnecessary rewording of the questions is not recommended.

Second, the questions are intended to guide the group toward understanding and applying the *main idea* of the passage. The author of the guide has stated his or her view of this central idea in the *purpose* of the study in the leader's notes. You should try to understand how the passage expresses this idea and how the study questions work together to lead the group in that direction.

There may be times when it is appropriate to deviate from the study guide. For example, a question may have already been answered. If so, move on to the next question. Or someone may raise an important question not covered in the guide. Take time to discuss it! The important thing is to use discretion. There may be many routes you can travel to reach the goal of the study. But the easiest route is usually the one the author has suggested.

7. Avoid answering your own questions. If necessary, repeat or rephrase them until they are clearly understood. An eager group quickly becomes passive and silent if they think the leader will do most of the talking.

8. Don't be afraid of silence. People may need time to think about the question before formulating their answers.

9. Don't be content with just one answer. Ask, "What do the rest of you think?" or "Anything else?" until several people have given answers to the question.

10. Acknowledge all contributions. Try to be affirming whenever possible. Never reject an answer. If it is clearly wrong, ask, "Which verse led you to that conclusion?" or again, "What do the rest of you think?"

11. Don't expect every answer to be addressed to you, even though this will probably happen at first. As group members become more at ease, they will begin to truly interact with each other. This is one sign of a healthy discussion.

12. Don't be afraid of controversy. It can be very stimulating. If you don't resolve an issue completely, don't be frustrated. Move on and keep it in mind for later. A subsequent study may solve the problem.

13. Stick to the passage under consideration. It should be the source for answering the questions. Discourage the group from unnecessary cross-referencing. Likewise, stick to the subject and avoid going off on tangents.

14. Periodically summarize what the *group* has said about the passage. This helps to draw together the various ideas mentioned and gives continuity to the study. But don't preach.

15. Conclude your time together with conversational prayer. Be sure to ask God's help to apply those things which you learned in the study.

16. End on time.

Many more suggestions and helps are found in *Leading Bible Discussions* (IVP). Reading and studying through that would be well worth your time.

Components of Small Groups

A healthy small group should do more than study the Bible. There are four components you should consider as you structure your time together.

Nurture. Being a part of a small group should be a nurturing and edifying experience. You should grow in your knowledge and love of God and each other. If we are to properly love God, we must know and keep his commandments (Jn 14:15). That is why Bible study should be a foundational part of your small group. But you can be nurtured by other things as well. You can memorize Scripture, read and discuss a book, or occasionally listen to a tape of a good speaker.

Community. Most people have a need for close friendships. Your small group can be an excellent place to cultivate such relationships. Allow time for informal interaction before and after the study. Have a time of sharing during the meeting. Do fun things together as a group, such as a potluck supper or a picnic. Have someone bring refreshments to the meeting. Be creative!

Worship. A portion of your time together can be spent in worship and prayer. Praise God together for who he is. Thank him for what he has done and is doing in your lives and in the world. Pray for each other's needs. Ask God to help you to apply what you have learned. Sing hymns together.

Mission. Many small groups decide to work together in some form of outreach. This can be a practical way of applying what you have learned. You can host a series of evangelistic discussions for your friends or neighbors. You can visit people at a home for the elderly. Help a widow with cleaning or repair jobs around her home. Such projects can have a transforming influence on your group.

For a detailed discussion of the nature and function of small groups, read *Small Group Leaders' Handbook* or *Good Things Come in Small Groups* (both from IVP).

Study 1. Parable of the Sower. Matthew 13:1-23.

Purpose: To understand the nature of parables and to examine what kind of soil we are.

Question 1. Almost every study begins with an "approach" question, which is meant to be asked before the passage is read. These questions are important for several reasons.

First, they help the group to warm up to each other. No matter how well a group may know each other, there is always a stiffness that needs to be overcome before people will begin to talk openly. A good question will break the ice.

Second, approach questions get people thinking along the lines of the topic of the study. Most people will have lots of different things going on in their minds (dinner, an important meeting coming up, how to get the car fixed) that will have nothing to do with the study. A creative question will get their attention and draw them into the discussion.

Third, approach questions can reveal where our thoughts or feelings need to be transformed by Scripture. This is why it is especially important not to read the passage before the approach question is asked. The passage will tend to color the honest reactions people would otherwise give because they are of course supposed to think the way the Bible does. Giving honest responses to various issues before they find out what the Bible says may help them to see where their thoughts or attitudes need to be changed.

Question 2. The Middle East was dominated by a rural, agricultural peasant culture.

Questions 3-4. D. A. Carson helps us understand these difficult verses: "It is naive to say Jesus spoke them [the parables] so that everyone might more easily grasp the truth, and it is simplistic to say that the sole function of parables to outsiders was to condemn them.

If Jesus simply wished to hide the truth from outsiders, he need never have spoken to them. His concern for mission . . . excludes that idea. So he must preach without casting his pearls before pigs (7:6). He does so in parables: i.e., in such a way as to harden and reject those who are hard of heart and to enlighten—often with further explanation—his disciples" (*Matthew*, p. 309).

Thus, hearing the parables does not cause a hard heart. Rather, having a hard heart causes one to not understand the parables. In this way the prophecy is fulfilled. "Otherwise," that is, if they did not have hard hearts, "they might see with their eyes, hear with their ears, understand with their hearts and turn, and I would heal them" (Mt 13:15).

Remember that the crowd is a mixture of devoted followers, of those mildly interested and perhaps drawn by curiosity and even of religious leaders who oppose Jesus. The mystery of the parable is revealed to those who want to know Jesus so much that they will follow up with questions when they don't understand something he says. The meaning of parables is hidden from those who do not want deeper spiritual understanding.

Robert Mounce (*Matthew*, Harper & Row, 1985, p. 128) also suggests that "at this point in his ministry Jesus deliberately adopted the parabolic method (cf. 13:34) in order to withhold, from those who did not believe, further truth about himself and the Kingdom he was bringing in. Since the knowledge of truth carries with it the responsibility of acceptance and appropriate action, the withholding of truth from those who were hardened against it should be interpreted as a desire not to increase judgment."

Question 8. In the second part of this question it might be helpful for the group to consider how they are tempted to respond to troubles or persecutions that arise because of their faith. This will help them to see more clearly how to avoid these temptations.

Questions 12-13. The parable challenges us to consider what kind of soil we are. But even if we are one of the first three types of soil, Jesus desires for us to become good soil that bears a crop. Encourage the group to give specific examples of how we can be responsive to God's Word.

Study 2. The Lost Sheep, the Lost Coin and the Lost Son. Luke 15:1-32.

Purpose: To grasp the Father's joyful acceptance of repentant sinners like us.

Question 1. It may not seem fair to some group members to have to choose between the words in each pair. Sometimes neither word may seem appropriate—or both may. But ask them which notion is stronger in their minds and why that is. Encourage them to speak their minds and not to say what they "ought" to say.

Question 2. The Pharisees were noted for their exact observance of religion, their exacting exposition of the law and their adoption of many extrabiblical customs and traditions. The teachers of the law, or scribes, were a class of lay interpreters of the Torah who generally allied themselves with the Pharisees on doctrinal issues.

"Tax collectors" were Jews who collaborated with the occupying Roman forces by gathering the taxes required by Rome. Thus they were usually ostracized from Jewish social circles.

Question 4. For example, we can imagine the shepherd anxiously counting and recounting his sheep, then carefully searching the surrounding hill country. Some artists have captured the beautiful image of him joyfully returning home with the lost sheep on his shoulders. Then there is the celebration in heaven! (Angels singing and shouting for joy?) Encourage the group to use their imaginations, and they will get much more out of all three parables.

Question 5. The common elements in these three parables make clear that Jesus is making the same point in each one.

Question 8. Obviously the Pharisees would strongly object to the son's squandering his wealth and his wild living. Notice, however, the other offensive elements of the story. Normally, the sons did not receive their inheritance until the father's death—although this story obviously indicates there were exceptions to this rule. The "distant country" was probably outside of Jewish territory, so the son was living with Gentiles—"dogs," as the Jews referred to them. In addition, he was feeding pigs, animals which Jews were forbidden to eat and which no self-respecting Jew would ever own as livestock. Finally, the son sank so low that he even ate the pigs' food himself! Give the group time to discover many of these details on their own, but feel free to mention any items they omit.

Question 12. The emphasis of all three parables is the Father's attitude toward repentant sinners. But the third parable can be viewed from two perspectives, that of the younger son and that of the older son. The younger son represents the tax collectors and "sinners" who were gathering around Jesus. It assures such people that the Father joyfully accepts those who repent. The older son represents the Pharisees and teachers of the law. The parable challenges their condemning, self-righteous attitude by urging them to view "sinners" from the Father's perspective. But notice that the father pursues the older son and extends his mercy to him despite his pharisaic sin. The question Jesus now poses to the Jewish leaders is, Who is really the lost son? The Father has come out to talk to the older son, searching for him as it were, seeking to bring him back.

Study 3. The Good Samaritan. Luke 10:25-37.

Purpose: To understand what it means to be a neighbor to those around us.

Question 3. In verse 28 Jesus tells the man, "You have answered correctly." Most of us would have said, "You have answered incorrectly! No one can inherit eternal life by obeying the law. You must have faith in Jesus Christ." Encourage the group to wrestle with how this seemingly incorrect and unscriptural answer can be "correct."

Question 4. Almost any system of religious rules is too much for any person to follow 100% of the time.

Question 5. Walter L. Liefeld tells us: "The distance from Jerusalem to Jericho is about seventeen miles, descending sharply toward the Jordan River just north of the Dead Sea. The old road, even more than the present one, curved through rugged, bleak, rocky terrain where robbers could easily hide. It was considered especially dangerous, even in a day when travel was normally full of hazards" (*Luke,* The Expositor's Bible Commentary, vol. 8, ed. Frank E. Gaebelein [Grand Rapids, Mich.: Zondervan, 1984], p. 943).

Question 6. In order to feel the impact of this parable, we must understand how the expert in the law would have viewed each of the central characters in the story. Priests were descendants of Aaron who served in the temple and offered sacrifices. Levites were descendants of Levi (but not Aaron) who assisted in temple services. The expert in the law might have expected such religious men to help the one on the side of the road. (They were returning from Jerusalem, so they were not in danger of ritual defilement if the man happened to be dead.) Today the name *Samaritan* refers to one who does good. But in Jesus' day the Samaritans were hated by the Jews and, no doubt, by this expert in the law. He could love his Jewish neighbors, but felt no obligation to love people of the despised Samaritan race.

Questions 8-9. Remember that parables are designed to overturn our existing ideas and to bring forth new ways of thinking and acting. Encourage the group to explore how the parable might have had this effect on the expert in the law.

Study 4. The Unforgiving Servant. Matthew 18:15, 21-35.

Purpose: To understand why it is essential that we forgive others.

Question 3. The disciples were known for their squabbles. It is entirely possible that Peter, given his strong, action-oriented personality, had someone in particular in mind.

Question 4. Some Rabbinic teaching of the time held that forgiving someone three times was all that the law required. Peter extends it to the number symbolizing perfection, seven.

Question 5. Some translations have "seventy times seven," but seventy-seven is a more accurate translation. Either way, however, Christ's point is the same.

Question 8. Whether the sum is millions of dollars or a few dollars, forgiveness is costly. But the cost of our forgiving others is nothing compared to God's forgiving us.

Questions 10-11. There are times when each of us has difficulty forgiving others. Problems arise, however, when we persist in being critical and unforgiving. During such times we need a fresh appreciation for God's mercy toward us. Those who continually refuse to forgive others demonstrate that they are strangers to God's forgiveness.

Question 12. Be sure to leave time for prayer. This can be a time of thankfulness and praise as well as a time of personal healing.

Study 5. The Widow and the Judge. Luke 18:1-8.

Purpose: To show us why we should always pray and not give up.

Question 3. It is important in parables and in narrative literature to use our imagination. Unless we see, feel and vicariously experience what is described, we will not be able to fully interpret and apply what we read.

Question 9. In order to understand this parable, we must recognize the kind of comparison Jesus intends us to make between the judge and God. It is an argument from the lesser to the greater, what rabbis sometimes referred to as "the light and the heavy." If the judge was such an uncaring person and he granted the widow's request, then *how much more* will a loving and just God answer our prayers! This is not quite the same as saying God is similar to or different from the judge.

Questions 10-13. The desperate situation of believers in the last times is made clear by the intensity of their prayers described in verse 7. Such apparent suffering could dampen the faith of many. In other passages of Scripture we are told that the world will go through intense tribulation before the Lord's return. In Matthew 24:12, for example, Jesus tells us that "because of the increase of wickedness, the love of most will grow cold." Circumstances may look so bleak and hopeless that believers will be tempted to give up hope. But Jesus encourages us by promising that "he who stands firm to the end will be saved" (Mt 24:13). His assurance applies not only to the final moments of history but to any trials or difficulties we experience as his followers.

Study 6. The Wheat and the Weeds. Matthew 13:24-30, 36-43.
Purpose: To understand why God allows good and evil to coexist in the world.

Question 2. The weeds sown by the enemy were probably darnel, which looks like wheat when it is young but looses its similarity when the heads of grain appear on the wheat. Notice, however, that in the parable the wheat has already sprouted and formed heads, making it clearly distinguishable from the weeds (v. 26). The owner doesn't forbid separating the two because the servants might mistake wheat for weeds but rather because they might "root up the wheat with them" (v. 29). As the two plants grew together, their roots would have become entangled, making it impossible to pull up the one without the other.

Question 8. Church history records several unfortunate attempts to pull up the weeds prematurely. The Crusades and the Spanish Inquisition are two of the most notable.

Question 9. The early church fathers, Augustine and the Reformers understood this parable as applying to genuine and counterfeit Christians within the church. According to this view, the parable warns us against trying to purify the church, since this could lead to excommunicating genuine believers and since separation will occur at the end of the age.

However, Jesus tells us in verse 38 that the field is the *world,* not the church. Likewise, it is not a case of mistaken identity between the weeds and the wheat. Rather the issue is that pulling out one can result in pulling out the other. Christians (the sons of the kingdom) are to live together with non-Christians (the sons of the evil one) in the world until the final judgment.

In other words, the parable does not address the subject of church discipline or imply that we should not exercise church discipline for fear of tearing the whole church apart. Rather, the question here is why God does not immediately uproot evil in the world.

Study 7. The Parable of the Vineyard Workers. Matthew 19:16—20:16.

Purpose: To understand that human values of fairness and worth are sometimes the opposite of kingdom values.

Question 2. It has occasionally been claimed that Jesus is denying his own goodness in verse 17 and is therefore implying that he is sinful. Notice, however, that he does not comment on whether he shares in God's goodness. He is not seeking to deny or confirm his divinity in this passage. His point in asking the question focuses on the young man's inadequate understanding of goodness. The man needs to realize that "in the absolute sense of goodness required to gain eternal life, only God is good" (Carson, *Matthew,* p. 422).

Questions 3-4. In order to understand this dialog between Jesus and the rich young man, we must be sensitive to the approach Jesus is taking. The man wants to know what *he* can do to get (earn?) eternal life. Jesus answers him on that level, telling him that only those whose goodness is equal to God's, who keep his commandments because they share God's goodness, will enter life. Jesus knows the man has not kept the commandments in that sense, but the man does not yet know it, as his somewhat boastful and naive response indicates. He claims he has kept the sixth, seventh, eighth, ninth and fifth commandments (in that order), implying that he has kept *all* the commandments. When Jesus asks him to sell his possessions, he exposes the man's true spiritual condition. He has made money his god, and therefore has broken the first and second commandments, which forbid idolatry. Instead of admitting his sinfulness and need of God's grace, the young man goes away sad.

Jesus recognized that you can't offer salvation to someone who doesn't feel the need for any help. So he attempts to expose a sense of need by showing the compelling demand of all the commandments.

Question 5. It is sometimes claimed that there was a gate in Jerusalem named "the eye of a needle," and that camels could only pass through that gate with great difficulty. This idea has no basis in fact. Camels were the largest animals in Palestine, and "the eye of a needle" Jesus refers to is that of a sewing needle (extremely small by comparison). Jesus' point is that it is not only difficult but *impossible* (v. 26) for a camel to pass through the eye of a needle, just as it is impossible for us to be saved on our own. We must look to the God with whom "all things are possible" (v. 26).

Question 8. It is not that the landowner is being unfair to those who worked all day since he paid them fully and promptly what was promised and what they agreed to. Rather he is being generous to those who only worked an hour—something he has a full right to do with his own wealth.

Study 8. The Wise and Foolish Virgins. Matthew 24:36—25:13.
Purpose: To realize the importance of being ready for Christ's return.

Questions 2-6. The discussion of Noah as well as the three parables Jesus tells in this passage reinforce certain themes and focus on different aspects of those themes. For example, all emphasize that Christ's coming will be unexpected (vv. 24:36, 42, 44, 50; 25:13). Likewise, all emphasize that we should be ready (vv. 24:42, 44, 46; 25:10, 13). In addition, all express an event that normal people should fear rather than celebrate. However, the latter two parables begin to reveal not only the unexpectedness of Christ's return but also his long delay (24:48; 25:5). And the parable of the master and his servants stresses that we must be faithful stewards of the responsibilities God has given us.

Verses 40-41 are not clear about whether those taken away are taken in judgment or as the elect (though the surrounding stories of Noah, the thief and the master indicate judgment). In any case, the point is the unexpectedness of the event.

Question 3. These everyday activities may or may not be wrong. But when seen in the context of impending disaster, they show a woeful emphasis on the wrong things at the wrong time.

Question 5. The group may be tempted to suggest some spiritual meaning to "give them their food at the proper time" (v. 45), such as teaching and discipling other Christians. However, it is doubtful that

Jesus intended us to find significance in every element in this parable. The point is that our readiness means being faithful by being good stewards of whatever responsibility God has assigned to us. The New Testament spells out these responsibilities in great detail. Encourage members of the group to discuss some of these.

Questions 7-8. Notice that all of the virgins fell asleep (v. 5). Likewise, all probably had some oil in their lamps originally (v. 8). However, only the wise virgins took extra oil in jars along with their lamps and were therefore prepared for the bridegroom's long delay. Their refusal to let unwise virgins have some oil was not based on selfishness but on common sense. If everyone ran out of oil halfway through the procession, it would be a disaster.

In parables such as this one, it is very tempting to look for symbolism in each aspect of the story: What does the oil represent? Why are there five in each group? Why does the bridegroom come at midnight? Such details were likely not intended to communicate specific meanings but rather to add color and drama to the story to help enhance its main point.

Question 11. As you discuss how we can take Christ's warnings more seriously, be sure to realize that the kind of readiness Jesus speaks of determines whether a person enters or is excluded from God's kingdom (vv. 10-12). It *is* a matter of the utmost seriousness!

Study 9. Parable of the Talents. Matthew 25:14-30.

Purpose: To consider the issues of inequality and fairness in God's kingdom and the importance of being faithful in the responsibilities he has given us.

Question 2. A talent was worth approximately six thousand denarii, so it would take a day laborer twenty years to earn that much. In today's currency, a talent would be worth around $300,000. The other two servants would, therefore, have been entrusted with $1,500,000 and $600,000 respectively (Carson, *Matthew,* p.516).

Question 6. The "at once" of verse 16 indicates the conscientiousness of the first two servants in executing their responsibilities. The first two also felt secure enough in their relationship with their master to be willing to risk their portions in some business enterprise. The actions of the third servant reveal a very different attitude and relationship.

Notice that the master refers to the first two servants as not only "faithful" but "good" (vv. 21, 23). Likewise, the lazy servant is referred to as "wicked" (v. 26).

Question 11. As the group discusses the implications of the parable, be sure that they also consider the spiritual principle mentioned in verse 29, which summarizes the main thrust of the parable.

Study 10. The Pharisee and the Tax Collector. Luke 18:9-14.

Purpose: To realize why we should humble rather than exalt ourselves.
Question 2. Encourage the group to describe the people in verse 9 in their own words rather than merely reading the verse.
Question 4. The Pharisee did and gave more than what was required—and he knew it. The Law required fasting only on the Day of Atonement, but the Pharisees fasted twice a week. Likewise, the Law required a tithe on what people earned, but the Pharisees tithed from all they acquired.
Question 6. Notice that the tax collector, unlike the Pharisee, seeks to rely on God's mercy rather than on his own righteousness.
Question 9. It is difficult for this parable to have the same impact on us as it had on the original hearers. For one thing, we are used to thinking of the Pharisees as self-righteous hypocrites. But in the first century they were viewed as models of religious devotion. Tax collectors, on the other hand, were despised because they worked for the Romans who had conquered Palestine. Even though they were Jewish, they collected more than necessary from their countrymen in order to increase their own wealth. For these reasons, the conclusion to the story in verse 14 would have shocked those listening to Jesus. They would have expected exactly the opposite!

Study 11. Parable of the Rich Fool. Luke 12:13-21.

Purpose: To consider the dangers of greed and the importance of being spiritually rich.

Question 2. Notice that the man doesn't ask Jesus to decide what is just; he simply wants a decision to be rendered in his favor. We are not told whether the other brother had agreed to have Jesus judge the case. Jesus' reply indicates that the man had improper motives and priorities.

Question 3. Be sure to observe the words Jesus uses: "Watch out!" "Be on guard!" Evidently greed is a danger we must be alert for, an enemy we must guard against.

Questions 4-5. In some ways the man's actions were logical and appropriate, although we can detect a degree of self-centeredness in verses 16-18. In verse 19, which clearly reveals the man's attitude, we can detect his warped perspective.

Question 9. Notice that Jesus does not condemn all rich people in verse 21—only those who are not rich toward God. However, the issue is a bit more complex than a simple yes or no to this question, as the following questions indicate.

Study 12. The Rich Man and Lazarus. Luke 16:19-31.

Purpose: To realize the importance of listening to Scripture, especially its emphasis on being concerned for the needs of others.

Question 2. Even though Lazarus is named, which is quite unusual for a parable, it should not be assumed that Jesus is telling a story of actual people rather than a fictional account. It is remarkable, however, that this story and the account of Jesus' friend Lazarus in John 11 both deal with death, resurrection and the refusal of people to believe as a result of a resurrection.

In biblical times "*purple* was cloth dyed with a very costly dye (obtainable from the shellfish murex). It would be used for the outer garment and the *fine linen* for the undergarment. The combination stands for the ultimate in luxury" (Leon Morris, *The Gospel According to Luke,* Tyndale New Testament Commentaries, ed. R. V. G. Tasker [Grand Rapids, Mich.: Eerdmans, 1974], p. 252).

Although Lazarus longed to eat what fell from the rich man's table, there is no indication that he did so. Notice that even the dogs have greater compassion than the rich man, licking Lazarus's sores.

Question 5. Remember that the parables differ from plain teaching. This parable is not designed to give an accurate portrayal of heaven and hell, so much as to emphasize the importance of value judgments made in this life in light of their impact on the next.

Question 9. There is an unmistakable allusion to Christ's resurrection in verse 31. However, even this failed to convince those who had no interest in listening to God.

Question 11. As the group discusses these questions, be sure they notice verse 31. It points out that the key issue is listening "to Moses and the Prophets" and, by inference, the One who will rise from the dead.

John White is former associate professor of psychiatry at the University of Manitoba. He is a writer and speaker with a worldwide ministry. His many books include The Fight, Eros Defiled, Parents in Pain *and* Healing the Wounded *(with Ken Blue).*